"PRISON STARING YOU IN THE FACE"

TIFFANEY BARRETT

WESTBOW
PRESS®
A DIVISION OF THOMAS NELSON
& ZONDERVAN

Scripture taken from the King James Version of the Bible.

WestBow Press books may be ordered through booksellers or by contacting:

WestBow Press
A Division of Thomas Nelson & Zondervan
1663 Liberty Drive
Bloomington, IN 47403
www.westbowpress.com
1 (866) 928-1240

ISBN: 978-1-5127-3025-8 (sc)
ISBN: 978-1-5127-3026-5 (e)

Library of Congress Control Number: 2016902046

Print information available on the last page.

WestBow Press rev. date: 02/04/2016

-This Know Also, That In The Last Days

Perilous Times Will Come.

KJV 2 Timothy3:1

CONTENTS

ACHIEVEMENT BOULEVARD

All is going well. Life is grand. You have a daily regimen that is uninterrupted. School may be in your routine. Working towards a high school diploma, Ged, Associates Degree, Bachelors, Masters, or a PHD. Possibly you have obtained these goals. There are no disruptions whatsoever in your life. Employed by a company you absolutely love. Just became an entrepreneur or thinking about it. Perhaps you're paid salary. Your profession may be in sales, a professor, teacher, nurse, doctor, or a lawyer. Maybe you're a stay at home mom or dad.

If I missed your profession it applies to you as well.

Every area of your life is heartwarming.

WHAT CAUSES YOU TO THRIVE

I had to a look around me. I grew up in a small town where most people were satisfied with working an industrial job. Many got married to classmates. The contentment of living in what people would call a house on the hill with a white picket fence. That was not my story. Are you driven by family, bills, education, past failures? Do you feel you have an image to uphold? No one wants to quit. What will propel you into your next level of life?

TURBULENCE

Here comes disturbance, just when life was at its best. Yes, the odds are stacked against you. You had a picture perfect life. No one can ever find out. Oh God not me. I have to portray everything is always together with me. My wife/husband (boyfriend/girlfriend) doesn't love me anymore. My husband/wife boyfriend/girlfriend) is cheating on me. I'm married but feel unloved. In a relationship and treated unvalued. The cell phone has replaced intimate time.

My wife/girlfriend goes and comes as she pleases. Mostly interacts with single women, so therefore she wants to do what singles do. Married to man/women (boyfriend/girlfriend) that is unforthcoming about their personal business. You would think they worked for the Secret Services. We once did everything together, now it has become a problem. **WATCH that**. Phone rings he breaks for the door. This is the oldest trick in the book. I lost service. Husband/ boyfriend "Hello, hello, hello. I can't hear them". Phone rings continually I will just turn it off. Even better, they will silence it.

Oh Boy. Here we go. Kids are out of control. Gone to the doctor and you just got a negative report for you or a loved one. You received news of the death of someone close to you. In school and you just got a failing grade. Just got terminated from your job or laid off. Now, what do I do? The worst thing you can do is begin to exhibit unhealthy behavior or a negative attitude. Not me, this is not supposed to happen to me. Why not you? I understand why. Oh you think it's because you went to an Ivy League school. I grew up with both parents in the home. I wasn't an illegitimate child. A safe haven was created for hard times. If I lost my job I'm all right. House burns down I'm hunky-dory. If I have a change of heart about the relationship I'm in, I can jump ship. Impregnate someone or you become pregnant. Not ready, this can't be happening now.

Money saved to take multiple vacations. Okay you just want to throw in the towel. Just giving up on whatever you were doing or accomplishing. You are feeling overwhelmed. Well I got news for you giving up is not an option. In order to get to a new level in life; you must complete the level you are on. You have to encourage yourself sometimes.

Many times you will look and no one will be there for you. I know you have helped people. Maybe you were just a listening ear. Offered advice from your past experiences to let them know they will make it. Trust me I totally understand. Been there, I can attest to that. **KJV Exodus 33:14 And he said, my presence shall go with thee, and I will give thee rest.**

Don't know What To Do

You are in a venerable state at this point. You are unaware that you are craving happiness or seeking attention. So much turmoil is happening around you. Therefore you can't see clearly. It is significant that you do not hasten to make decisions during this time. Be very attentive in this uncertain season of your life. Making one wrong choice can cause you countless years to recover. **KJV Proverbs 3:5-6 "Trust in the Lord with all thine heart; and lean** not to thine own understanding. In all thy ways acknowledge him, and he shall direct thy paths.

THE DECEPTION

The trickery begins. You are now looking through the eyes of someone who has been shaking to the very core of their soul. This is where confusion creeps in. Instability will take root. Instability can be unreliability, insecurity, and unpredictability. So many things can fall under instability. This is when the enemy begins to strategize against you. Positioned in a state where you cannot discern what is to come. This makes you an open target for the enemy. The chaos has consumed you. You are in the eye of the storm. Your perception has become distorted. It's only an illusion. What you see is not what you are going to get. Be very, very cautious in this season.

COUNTERFEIT

I will tell you about my experience of a counterfeit.
After divorcing I moved to NYC. As a result of not
knowing what to do I moved to another state. One
Sunday I decided to go to church. During this time I
was reading my bible very little. In this season prayer
was scarce. Service this Sunday was awesome.
Leaving the house of God feeling revived.

After church I had a taste for some glazed
donuts. I decided to make a pit stop at Dunkin
Donuts. This was in the summer month. As I recall

it was almost 101 degrees this particular Sunday. I stopped in dunking donuts and got something to drink and ordered glazed donuts. I took a seat to enjoy my donuts. This guy walks up "Do you mind if I set here and eat? "He stated. "No, I don't". I replied. He takes a seat and we began to converse. "Hi my name is William". The gentlemen stated. "I'm Felicia" I replied. Discussing the temperature and how it was too hot to be outside. While conversing with the gentleman he could tell I was not a New Yorker. My accent revealed southerner all day. The conversation was enjoyable.

The pit stop turned into an hour and a half stop. Can we say distraction? Do you see what is happening? We exchanged phone numbers. We began to date. Not immediately after meeting. This person was a master manipulator. He knew how to act when placed in a specific environment. White collar environment could play the part to the tee.

Thug didn't have to pretend. What is in you will come out. KJV Luke 6:45 – A good man brings good things out of the good stored up in his heart, and an evil man brings evil things out of the evil stored up in his heart. For the mouth speaks what the heart is full of. Also, his rap sheet was extensive. This person was extremely arrogant. He was well off financially. William was seeking to purchase a house in the south. William asked me would if I would find a realtor and book an appointment. He also stated it didn't matter what state the home was in. William wanted to move out of New York. Whatever William purchased he paid cash for it.

Contacting a realtor in Georgia the appointment was scheduled for the following week. We took a trip to Georgia. Staying in a hotel for one week and looking at homes every day. Finally William found what he was looking for. The house had five bedrooms, four bathrooms, fully carpeted, and a finished basement. The basement had five rooms as well, all with carpet. This looked like another house downstairs. The house was on the lake in an upscale neighborhood. Upon returning back to New York I got a job in the medical field. Everything was peaches and cream in the relationship. Remember I told you earlier **it's only an illusion**.

PEOPLE ASSIGNED TO ABORT YOUR DESTINY

Slowly but surely I went to church less and less. This individual wanted to control every aspect of my life. William acted like he was mentally ill.

I was in a relationship that was unhealthy. I encountered a lot of nerve wrecking moments. The level of anger that was exhibited towards me was frightening. We traveled a great deal on a regular basis.

Some Sunday mornings I would attend church. Continually I sang worship music on a daily basis. This is how I would start my day. Praying aloud often and talking to God is something that I enjoy doing. I felt as if I had no one but God. Living in a different state and not having any friends or associates at the time. Here I am with an individual who is now proclaiming to be an agnostic. William's behavior was not pleasant on frequent occasions. Several trips were horrendous.

William was not pleased the way I prepared dinner. Becoming agitated I responded by saying whatever it's just an onion. It's all going the same way. He continued to scream at me. I yelled at him whatever. I was sitting at the kitchen table. He stood in the center of the kitchen at the island. I wish I could go into every detail. He smacked me so hard I fell onto the floor. Smacking me uncontrollably like a rag doll. Quickly running into the bathroom downstairs and locking the door.

Another occasion William invited a lifelong friend to come visit. A friend he had not seen in about 20 years. Jason and his girlfriend Kelly arrived on a Saturday morning. The day was very pleasant. As the night approached the discussion was made between Jason and Kelly they were going out on the town. So William decided that we would join the two. Everyone was sipping on some type of alcohol. I even took a few drinks myself. It was time to go. We arrived at the first sports bar/club.

Shortly after we arrived Kelly and I went to the restroom. As we exited the restroom, a man grabbed my hand. I quickly pulled away from him. He said something to me but I did not understand. Approaching William I could see a disturbing look on his face. He said to me "What did that dude say to you"? I told him I didn't understand what he said. My attention was refocused on William. Thinking everything was fine. I was soon to be in for a rude awaking. The guy that grabbed my hand earlier attempted to walk by us. If only he would have walked around the other side of the building. An altercation started before you could blink your eyes. We had no choice but to leave. I assumed we were headed home but the decision was made to make another stop. I sat soundlessly and very apprehensive to speak.

Drawing near the next club William showed euphoric emotions as if nothing happened. Before we went inside everyone wanted to take pictures. Present physically but mentally I was somewhere else. Proceeding to go inside William's behavior was superb. Realizing a retired professional basketball player stood near us. William was elated. Walking over to the retired player William asked him for his autograph and to take a picture. I took the picture. Standing there engaged in a conversation with the retired ball player. The night quickly came to an end.

Leaving the club I attempted to drive us home. Shortly, after leaving it was a disaster. You ran the light. You can only imagine the profanity spoken. Get out of the car. I was getting screamed at. As I got out of the car he came around use your imagination. It was definitely a night to remember. Get in the back. A car pulled up and the driver asked what is going on? They were told to mind their business. The driver pulled off. Jason got in the front and Kelly stayed in the back.

Kelly tried to console me. Both Jason and Kelly were terrified. No rationalizing could be done with this guy. As the car was driven you would have thought we were in a drag racing contest. Instantly the car came to a stop. Kelly jumped out and took off running. Jason ran after her. William started to do donuts in the road. The car was almost on two wheels. Saying to him please slow down you are going to kill us. He yelled back cursing me out. It's your fault we are in this. Eventually Jason and Kelly were picked up. Pulling into the driveway there was no end to this madness. Kelly came into the bedroom to console me. Downstairs William was on a rampage. Kelly said to me William is psychotic. If you don't leave him he is going to kill you. Sunday morning it was. I slept for about 2 hours and then called the neighbor and asked her if she wanted to go to church with me. She said yes. I told her everything that happened. Surprised by astonishment she could not believe her ears.

William portrayed to his Georgia neighbors an image of someone that had been to an Ivy League school. Came from a home an upper class family and was born into wealth. Not the case by any means. When I returned from church I did not say a word to anyone. Went to the bedroom and remained there until the next morning. William craved my attention all day. I gave him a look that spoke volumes. A look that said I have no liberty with you. **KJV Galatians 5:13 "For, brethren, ye have been called unto liberty for an occasion to the flesh, but by love serve on another.**

RICKERS EXPERIENCE

Life back in New York drained me mentally, physically and emotionally. I contemplated on how to depart from this damaging relationship. Living in an apartment we shared with William's cousin Paul and his girlfriend Shelia. Deciding I wanted to take a real-estate course. I found a course offered downtown Manhattan. Going downtown to register and pay for the class William did not want to go with me. On the way back home I got lost. When I arrived William said to me what took you so long. Telling him I got lost. He began to insult me. Telling me how stupid I was for getting lost.

I said look just let it go. Why did I say that! William just got out of the shower and was drying off when I walked in. As he continued cursing me out he began rolling the damp towel up; that he was drying off with. He took the towel stretched it with both hands and forcefully popped me between the eyes as hard as he could. Now William stood around six three and weighed around 290 pounds. Very muscular because he lifted weights systematically for years. His arms were like pythons. I screamed to the top of my lungs. Finding the closest thing to me was his cell phone. I threw it at him. Of course I missed him. Rushing me he hit me in my right leg with a closed fist so hard I blacked out.

I fell on the bed. The pain was so excruciating. Giving birth before the pain felt to be ten times worse. Trying to stand for hours I was unable to get up. William took my cell phone and left. Eventually I had to hop into the hallway hours later. Grunting and moaning because of the pain. Paul had some crutches behind the door. I began to use them. The pain that I felt afterwards was indescribable. Instantly a bruise formed the size of a cantaloupe.

The color was a deep dark purple. There was severe discoloration. It was so painful to get up and down. I could hardly walk. To use stairs was almost impossible. Getting in and out of the car I had to turn sideways. Not going to the hospital because I was afraid. About a week or so passed. William was on a rampage again. This time he was throwing my things into the hall. Telling me to get out and let's go. On many occasions William threatened me.

He told me he would kill me and my whole family. Shelia had company over during the altercation.

Running in the living room where they were. The expression on my face showed, help me. The visitor leaned over and she whispered do you want me to call the police. I said yes please hurry. She ran into the bathroom and called the police. I went behind her. William kicked the bathroom door open and the visitor she ran out of the bathroom. William came and stood over me and said if you don't get out I'm going to break your neck. I acted as if I was packing my things in the hall. Paul came out of the room and said to him just leave her alone man. William walks up to Paul looking him in the eye. Mind your business before I break your jaw. Everyone was petrified of William. He was like a ticking time bomb. William refocused his attention on me. Yelling lets go I'm not going to tell you again. William was in the dark the police were on their way. Boom, boom, Boom! I snatched to door open. Basically I fell into the officers arms. Help! Help! I yelled. Six officers were in the hallway. The officer said what is going on? Let's walk down the hall away from the apartment door the officer said. I proceeded to tell him. The officer said to me "show me your leg".

Whoever called in to make this complaint said your boyfriend hit you in your leg a week ago is that true "Yes" I replied. I showed him my leg he began to use profanity. The officer called his partners over. Take a look at what that guy did to her leg. One of his partners put his hand over his mouth. Two officers were standing in the hallway surrounding William. The officers acted as though they were scared of William. One officer said to William put your hands behind your back you are under arrest. William said to the officers "if I don't what are you going to do"?

William refusing will force us to go there the officer stated. He cooperated and put his hands behind his back. Felicia you have to go with us to the precinct.

When we arrived at the precinct walking in there was a fence that housed inmates. It served the purpose as a holding cell. William laid eyes on me when I walked in. Fear crippled me. I wanted to hide. Not wanting to see him. The officer took me in the back and informed a female officer of the situation. The male officer asked the female officer if she would take pictures of my leg. Part of the procedure I had to write an incident report. Immediately a restraining order was put in place against William. Upon leaving the precinct William starting screaming at me through the fence "See what you done. I'm in this situation because of you. Move my car so they don't tow it." Never looking back I continued to exit the building. An officer gave me a ride home.

William stayed locked up for 48 hours. When he was released he came back to the house. Of course he gave me a sob story. He cried like a baby and told me he needs help. Staying in the relationship was a mistake. God gave me a plan of escape. **KJV 1 Corinthians 10:13 "There hath no temptation taken you but such as is common to man: but God is faithful, who will not suffer you to be tempted above that ye are able; but will with the temptation also make a way to escape, that ye may be able to bear it."**

Shelia agreed she would help me pack my things. I came home from church and William was gone. Timing could not have been better. Packing everything I owned. I called my mom to see what she was doing. I never informed her of what was happening. So I continued packing my things. William had not returned yet. Getting a little nervous I called William to find out his location. I told William I wanted to go to the emergency room. Previously I was angry with William and was trying to leave so he laid on me. Squirming to get him off of me I pulled a muscle in my left side. The pain continued, three days past. Shelia and I took my things downstairs on the apartment complex. We lived on the third floor. Taking my things to the first floor and stashing everything under the stair case. William calls my cellphone "come on out I'm parked in front of the apartment".

Now the car that William was driving was registered to me. The title was in my name in the state of North Carolina. I had full coverage insurance on the car. The title was clear with no liens. I go out and get in on the passenger side. When I get in I don't close the door. I had my feet on the ground. We started conversing. It quickly turned into an argument. William started choking me. Not with his hands. He had my head pint down between the console and the seat of the car. He was chocking me with the back of his arm. William applied pressure to the center of my neck. This cut off my air supply. Taking my feet I began kicking the door, as if I were a madwoman.

Now the apartment was directly in front of a park. As I was kicking the door people were walking by. A man ran over yelling let her go. This drew a large crowd. William let me go. He gets out of the car and left the key in the ignition. I get out and I'm crying frantically. Someone please call the police. William is standing in front of the car. I run around the back of the car and jumped in the driver's seat.

Starting the car up and putting it into reverse. When William realized I was leaving he starting running towards the car. I was backing up so fast the car was whining. William runs to the front passenger side of the car and hits the window. His punch was so powerful the windshield blow out. This was as if someone removed the windshield. Not a piece of glass remained. All the glass was in the front seat and in my lap.

I got away. My things were back at the apartment Shelia called me to notify me that William left. She told me come get your things we will help you load them up. One of her friends was there and offered help. I returned back to the apartment to get my things. A few months prior to this I met a gentle man by the name of Tony whom was a police officer. He also was an elder in his church. Tony invited me on several occasions to his church. We exchanged telephone numbers. Thank God I did. I thought about him at that moment. Pulling over before I approached the apartment. I called him and told him what happened. He said I'm on my way and stay put until I get there. Tony arrived and followed my back to the apartment. I called Shelia to let her know I was pulling up. Shelia and her friend came out right away with Storage containers. We all pitched in and loaded the car up. Tony told me to follow him. We drove a couple of blocks away from the apartment. Tony pulls over and I get out of the car and walk over to the driver's side of his car. Looking me in my eyes and advising me to press charges. I was very adamant about not wanting to follow through with that process. Continuing to persuade me why I should. My decision was made not to go. Fearful that William would hunt me down. Tony said what is your plan? Do you have somewhere you can stay tonight? No, I don't. The offer was made for me to stay at his apartment because he would not be home. Tony would be working third shift at a security job. I felt I would be safe because this guy was a police officer.

I agreed that I would and accepted his offer. Staying at Tony's place was very uncomfortable. This guy was someone I didn't know much about. Not knowing if William was able to locate me. Therefore I was unable to sleep that night. Up and down all night. I made sure I stayed away from the windows. Frightened that William would shot the house up.

Waking up the next morning I was exhausted. It was around eight in the morning. My phone rings. Hello I responded. I need to speak with Ms. Roles. Speaking! This is detective Bill. William Cane has made a complaint against you. He stated you stole his car, cell phone, Xbox, and keys to his home in Georgia.

The detective informed me I had to come into the precinct. I got in touch with Tony and told him about the call. He said to me I told you to press charges to cover yourself. I showed him the title to the car and my proof of insurance. Tony said you should be fine. Going down to the precinct alone probably wasn't the best thing to do. Arriving at the precinct I asked for detective Bill. He came right out. Follow me he stated. We entered a room full that was surrounded by glass.

Have a seat the detective said to me. He said let's get to the point. Another detective walks in I'm detective James. So William said you stole his car. I said I have my car title and my proof of insurance in my purse. William once owned the car but he no longer does. William and I both went to the NC DMV and had everything switched over into my name. Giving him all my documents he went and made copies. Also calling the North Carolina DMV and confirming the car title was legit. Well this all checks out but what about William's cell phone, Xbox and house keys. I said the Xbox belongs to me. I brought it from a friend of mine. His keys and cellphone are packed up. I removed everything out of the car last night. I did not steal anything. When I pulled off I was not about to check and see if William left anything in the car. I felt my life was in danger.

The two detectives left me in the room. About twenty minutes past. The detectives returned and said to me "We have to place you under arrest." Panic-stricken crying and responded how are you arresting me? Well William filed a report so we have to take action. It is up to the judge during trial to find you guilty or not. The detective said you are entitled to two phone calls. So I called an associate from real estate school that I had become close to Sarah and Tony. Sarah came to the precinct and I had her to call my mom. She was kind enough to take my documents to my mom. Tony came to the precinct but the detectives advised him not to get involved. This could compromise his job as a police officer.

This process took approximately six hours. Now we will read you your rights and take you downtown Manhattan to be processed. Placing the hand cuffs on me I felt as though I were floating. This did not seem like reality. Upon walking out the detective that joined detective Bill and I later began to say to me "I believe I know you. Didn't you come here before because of problems with your car in the past?" No, this is my first time ever coming in about a car. He replied "Yes you did." Not a word spoken from me. I was placed in the back seat.

Upon driving away detective Bill stops at the store. Felicia would you like anything. No thank you! I'm fine. Arriving at the courthouse downtown I felt fear setting in on me. Notifying me I had to see the District Attorney. Detective Bill informed me that the DA would interview me. The Da said to me "Do you give us permission to record you." Yes, I do. I had nothing to hide. I explained the entire situation to the District Attorney. This had no effect on me being released. After the interview was over I was taking to the back to be processed.

In the state of New York court continues around the clock. Court never closes. Doesn't matter what hour it is. Only on holiday's court closes. I was taking into the court room. The judge calls my name. "How will you be represented?" I would like a court appointed lawyer please. Immediately a lawyer was appointed to me. Attorney John Wayne comes and introduces himself. Felicia come with me. So Felicia here is the situation. You are being charged with Grand larceny, Grand Theft, Robbery, and Harassment. When I heard this I went mute. Felicia, Felicia Attorney Bill trying to get my attention. He continued speaking but I tuned him out. Felicia please say something. Looking at your criminal record it is clean other than speeding tickets. Felicia I am looking at William's criminal report. How on earth did you get involved with this villain? William is a dangerous person. I have some news it's not good. Do you have someone that can put up a bond for you? Maybe a house or some land. The problem is you are considered to be a nonresident. In order to be a resident in NYC you had to reside here six months or more. If not the judge is not going to release you.

I called Sarah and Tony again. Attorney Wayne said Felicia I feel for you. I believe you. The Attorney let me use his cell phone multiple times. Attorney Wayne said to me "Felicia call you mother". I have to go with another client but here is my number to the office and my cell number. I was sitting next to a gentle man while waiting for the judge to call me. The gentle leans over and said to me "You are from down south right". Yes, I am. "What are you doing here?" The gentleman asked. I briefly told him. I'm going to tell you this. If you don't get someone to bond you out soon. This is how the process works. Every two hours a bus will come and take people who have been sentenced or awaiting bond to Rickers Island. I said Rickers who. You mean Rickers

Island that they did a movie about. He said yes. The gentleman looked at mean and said I know you don't belong here.

Attorney Wayne informed me a bond had been set for me. Shortly after that I was taken to the back and placed in a holding cell. A pay phone was on the wall. There were about fifteen other women in the holding cell. I had about twenty dollars on me but I needed change. Asking around no one seemed to have change. Finally an officer said I will go get you change. I finally called my mother. Now I really had not spoken to her in a few months. I did not want to involve anyone in what I was dealing with. This is the worst thing you can do is isolate yourself away from everyone.

Getting through to my mom I telling her what was going on. I gave her the information about bonding me out. God worked it out where my mom was unable to bond me out. Sometimes God will allow you to stay in the storm so you will understand it was all God not man who got you out. This is what draws you closer to the Father. Hanging up the phone with her I began to pray Lord strengthen me for this and I trust you it will all work out.

The officer came to the cell and said Roles come with me. She said to me I'm placing you in the cell over here. It was in the back of the building the cell was humongous. I was alone in the cell. I started praying and talking to God. God gave me such a peace. **KJV Philippians 4:7 And the peace of God, which passeth all understanding, shall keep your hearts and minds through Christ Jesus.**

An hour or so passed. The officer came back and said Roles lets go. It's Time to go. The bus has arrived to transport inmates to Rickers. I was unbothered when we were loading the bus. Since this was my first time going to Rickers the officer informed me that it was policy that I would sit alone. This space was so confined. Imagine a seat in a go-cart. Well this seat was about the width of that. Envision cell bars around it. There was a door that closed and locked once you were seated. Then I was hand cuffed and shackled. At the time I was claustrophobic I began to panic and gasp for air. The officer opened the door and patted me on the back it's going to be alright. I closed my eyes and began praying and singing worship songs.

Pulling in at Rickers the one officer went in the building. There were two officers that rode the bus with twenty five or so inmates. It took about one hour for them to start unloading all the inmates off of the bus. As we were escorted inside the prison

I was in disbelief what I seen. All twenty five or so inmates were placed in a large cell. A bench surrounded the entire wall of the cell. A metal toilet was in the corner with no privacy. Just in the open space. This cell could probably house seventy inmates. People were lying on the nasty floor because there wasn't a place to sit. It smelt really bad. Discovering some women had been in this cell waiting to be moved five or six hours.

My named was called with a group of other women. We were taken to another department where you had to remove all clothes and be searched. You are also given the option to take a shower. Next you were taken to another department where you were examined by a doctor and have an Aids test administered. The results are instant. After this process you are taken to another department and you are given a mat and some personal supplies.

The final step to this entire process is that you are assigned a bunk. Now this department looked new. It looked like a dorm with maybe fifty or sixty beds. Not sure how many beds. I felt a little better when I saw it was an open space and the facility looked clean. It even smelt like disinfectants. A desk was at the front room. An officer sat at the desk where she had a view of each inmate. I went to the precinct that morning. The time now was probably three in the morning.

So exhausted I made my bunk and went to sleep. You are woken up very early to eat breakfast. I think five in the morning. After you eat you can go back to bed. In order to make a phone call you have to have money in your account. You can only use the phone certain times. I called my mother. I informed her of my current situation. Everyone was issued a bible. It was almost like I was placed here to rest. You showered whenever you wanted too. In this dorm I began counseling people. Encouraging individuals letting them know Jesus loved them. Even began braiding hair. Thursday is when I arrived. I remained in Rickers until Tuesday the following week. On Tuesday morning I had court. The inmates were hugging me and crying because there was a chance I would not return. If you had court you were to be ready before four am that morning.

This was such a long and tedious process because so many people had court. Upon arriving at the courthouse we were giving instructions on what to do. As we exited the bus everyone was linked together with their handcuffs. Upon going inside the handcuffs were removed. You waited in a single line until your name was called. Roles come forward. I want you to follow the officer in front of you. I followed her and she took me to a holding cell that had fifteen other women there awaiting court. While waiting some of the women began to converse asking one another why are they there. When it was my time I told them. Then I followed to say I don't care what it looks like I believe God.

Women began to ask me to pray with them. One lady said to me "You are facing all of that and you have that kind of faith". I said to all of them this is only a test for me. One young lady I prayed for God told me to tell her she was going home. I also said the sinner's prayer with her. She gave her life to Christ. She thought she was going to be sentenced to prison. The officer called her next. She came back about forty five minutes later. She was crying uncontrollably. Running straight to me and hugging me. Thank you she replied. Please keep me in your prayers they dismissed my charges. Immediately when everyone heard this they were lined up for me to pray for them.

Roles come with me. The officer had in his hand some paperwork. Here is your court date. You are free to go. I never made it into the courtroom. Don't tell me God is not good. Later speaking to my Attorney he informed me that the DA is willing to drop the charges and seal your case. This is under the condition that you give William the car. Return his cell phone, Xbox, and his keys. Agree not to harass him and your case would be sealed. Taking my mom's advice I agreed to the conditions the DA made. The District Attorney kept her word. **KJV Blessed are ye, when {men} shall revile you, and persecute {you}, and shall say all manner of evil against you falsely, for my sake.**

THE COVERING OF GOD

Through this entire ordeal God had his hand on me. I was wrong in so many ways.

Just read the Ten Commandments in KJV. Read all of Exodus 20. I thank God for his grace and his mercy. There is no way I would have made it without God. This was a painful experience. A ministry was birth from this experience. People need to be real and tell their testimonies. I mean that thing that brought you embarrassment. That thing that almost left you crippled mentally and physically.

Psalms KJV 1 Have mercy upon me, O God, according to thy lovingkindness: according unto the multitude of thy tender mercies blot out my transgressions.

2 Wash me thoroughly from mine iniquity, and cleanse me from my sin.

Romans 8:28 And we know that all things work together for good to them that love God, to them who are the called according to his purpose.

Remember this you are an overcomer.

Printed in the United States
By Bookmasters